Proclaiming Liberty

Isaiah 61:1 and Luke 4:18

Overcoming Spiritual Hindrances
and Proclaiming Your Liberty

by
Frank S. Walb

God Bless You
F. Walb

xulon PRESS

Acknowledgements

I want to give thanks to our Heavenly Father for allowing me to write this book, and I give Him the Glory for all the Fruits and Blessings that Christians may receive while reading it.

I believe I was directed by God's Holy Spirit to write this book, and I pray it will accomplish God's highest Will in helping the Body of Christ to have a closer relationship with Jesus Christ and to be more powerful in the Holy Spirit to accomplish the tasks that He has for each of us.

I thank my Father God for blessing me with my wonderful Spirit-filled Christian wife who has supported and prayed for me through many trials and tribulations that I have gone through in our forty-one years of marriage. It's a blessing of the Lord to have a spouse who is in one accord with you when you pray and minister together for Christians who are hurting, and to see the changes in their lives. God has blessed us in so many ways ... and we praise Him for it!

I also give thanks to my friends, Sheila Niemela for assistance in editing, and Jimmy Stewart and the staff of the Xulon Press who helped me with the information required for writing this book.

Contents

ChapterPage

Introduction

I believe God has shown me a need in the Body of Christ for Spirit-filled Christians who are having problems overcoming thoughts in their mind that Satan uses to harass them and, therefore, hinders them from becoming strong in the Spirit. Our mind is the battleground — and that's the area where Satan tries to rob us from being strong, Spirit-filled Christians and preventing us from accomplishing what the Lord wants to do.

It is my hope and prayer that the words in this book be anointed by God and used to help Spirit-filled Christians overcome things in their past that Satan uses to rob them of their blessings.

When we come to the Lord and accept Him as our Savior … confess our sins … and repent of them, we are forgiven of all sins that we committed in our past; but sometimes we need God's healing and deliverance over certain things that have happened to us in our past that hinder us from progressing spiritually.

We have found that a number of Christians in the Body of Christ may have matured spiritually and with knowledge of God's Word, and want to move on with the Lord, but still have trouble with thoughts of things that happened to them in their past which they haven't been able to overcome. Although they pray and ask God to help them, they can't seem to fully overcome these things, so they can't continue on in their spiritual growth.

We can have Jesus as Lord over most of our life, but are unable to make Him Lord over some of these areas due to the hindrances in our past and thoughts that Satan bombards us with.

God forgives us for all of our sins, but *Satan is the accuser of the brethren* and uses certain things in our past to make us feel guilty and to keep us from being free spiritually. His intent is to rob us of our salvation, which he might do, if we continue to listen to his accusations and brain washing. The battlefield is in our minds and, if we listen to these accusations long enough, we start to agree with him; he, in turn, robs us and tries to kill us spiritually ... and physically ... if he can. *Satan is a thief and a robber* and has come to rob and destroy the Body of Christ! When we are free in the Spirit, we are much more powerful in our prayer life and are more effective in using our God-given spiritual authority to overcome him.

We have found that Satan uses many ways to hinder us from getting free and overcoming weak areas in our lives. He especially uses **Pride and Fear** because most people don't want others to know anything about their personal life and are fearful to ask someone else to pray for them. They want to look good in the eyes of others, so they put on a front to make other people believe that everything in their life is fine with no problems. They are afraid that the information they share would be gossiped about to others and make them look bad.

My prayer is that this information will help **Spirit-filled Christians** take control of their own lives and use their own God-given authority (given to us in Luke 10:19) to overcome these things from their past without having to go to someone else for help, and eliminating the fear of having to do so. However, I must say that sometimes it is more effective to go to another Christian whom you can trust, and pray together to receive this help, as it is expressed in James 5:15, 16. *Confess your trespasses to one another, and pray for one another that you may be healed.*

There is much more prayer power when two people are praying together in one accord, especially when there is a need to take authority against Satan's evil spirits. Although we have God's authority when we use the Name of Jesus Christ, we have found that numerous Christians fail to use their authority even though they may have the knowledge, either because of fear and unbelief …or just plain apathy.

With our intellect, it is hard to believe in spirits that we can't see, but God is Spirit, and the spirit world is real and much more powerful, and controls the physical world in which we live. When we pray, it starts God's angels into action in the spirit world to answer our prayers, but sometimes, if there is a spiritual problem, we also have to take authority over Satan's evil spirits that hinder our prayers from being answered. An example of this would be that if we were policemen who failed to take our authority to arrest criminals, they would be free to do whatever they wanted to do. Another example would be if we were to receive an inheritance, but did not use it, we would gain nothing from it.

For Christians to be able to walk with the Lord and overcome all the things Satan throws at us, we must use the authority that Jesus gave us to overcome him and his evil spirits. We can silently pray to God, but when we speak to Satan's evil spirits, we must *speak audibly, commanding them in the Name of Jesus Christ* to get out of us, our spouse, our children, etc. Remember, Jesus is the One who defeated Satan, and we must use His Name when we are in a spiritual battle with our enemy.

PREPARATION
PRAYER

For assuredly I say to you, whoever says to this mountain, be removed and be cast into the sea, and does not doubt in his heart, but believes that those things he says will come to pass, he will have whatever he says. Therefore I say to you, whatever things you ask when you pray, believe that you receive them, and you will have them. Mark 11:23-24

You should start with prayer giving thanks to God for all the blessings He has given to you. We fail to thank God for many things He does because we sometimes accept them as normal things in life, or things that we have done for ourselves. When we give thanks to God for everything, we are actually giving Him the Glory for doing them.

Commit yourself to God, ask God's Holy Spirit to show you those things in your lives that are unpleasing to Him (Psalms 139:23, 24), and ask for God's help to overcome those things that are hindering your spiritual growth and your ability to have Jesus as Lord of these areas in your lives.

Some Christians don't receive answers to their prayers because of doubt and unbelief in their hearts. They want to believe, and do believe in their minds, but have doubt and unbelief in their hearts. Also, in different Christian circles, I hear a lot of prayers that are prayed asking Jesus to do things that He has already done. When Jesus was hanging on the Cross before He died, He said, *"It is finished,"* which means that everything that He came to do for us on earth was completed.

Jesus gave each of us His authority to overcome the works of the devil (Luke 10:19), but we fail to use this authority — sometimes because of our unbelief or fear Satan and the unknown, so we continue to ask God to do it for us. Satan will do anything he can to keep us from using the authority Jesus gave us to overcome things that hinder our Christian walk. His purpose is to kill us spiritually or physically, or to hinder us so we will be ineffective in our Christian walk, in ministering and in helping others in the Body of Christ. God loves us and wants to establish a close relationship with us. He wants us to communicate with Him more often and to make Him the Lord of all the areas of our lives. There is no set way to pray your commitment to God, but the following "example" may help.

Sample Prayer: *Father God, I come to You in the precious Name of Your Son, and my Lord Jesus Christ, thanking You for all the blessings You have bestowed on me; and I praise You for Your love and concern for me. Lord God, I am asking for Your help in overcoming things in my life that hinder me from establishing a closer relationship with You. I commit myself to You and ask Your Holy Spirit to search deep within me and show me those things that are unpleasing to You. I know I was forgiven for my sins when I repented of them and asked You into my heart and for Your forgiveness, but I am still having trouble in certain areas that hinder me from getting closer to You. Lord Jesus, I thank You for Your love and concern for me, for giving Your life for my salvation, and for shedding Your blood so that I could be forgiven for all my sins. I commit my mind to You and bring it under the obedience of Christ Jesus (2 Corinthians 10:5) and in Jesus' Name, I ask for your help and direction to overcome these hindrances. I take authority over all evil spirits that exalt themselves against the knowledge of God, and I bind them and render them inactive in me... in Jesus' Name.*

Just remember this is only a **sample prayer**, and as you establish a closer relationship with the Lord, you will begin to feel free to pray to God in the way that seems right for you. The battle with these evil spirits is already won and we don't have to be afraid of them. We don't have to fight them, but we do have to *take authority over them, in the Name of Jesus Christ,* telling them to leave us, and they have to leave. Also one of the scriptures that we sometimes overlook is Mark 16:18, which tells us that one of the "signs of a believer" is *casting out evil spirits.* However, a huge number of Christians, through the lack of knowledge, don't use this God-given authority over Satan to get him out of their lives. (Hosea 4: 6) *My people are destroyed for lack of knowledge.* We as Christians don't realize how much Spiritual power we possess when we *pray or use the Name of Jesus to get Satan out of out lives*; therefore, we are robbed of many of our God-given blessings.

Problems that Hinder Us

As you pray and ask God to show you the things that hinder your Spiritual walk with Him, wait and listen to God's Holy Spirit as He searches your inner being showing you areas that you should look at in your life. Most people already know what troubles them, but sometimes don't realize there may be areas from their past which are hindering their spiritual growth. These could be areas that they may feel uncomfortable to look at and, in some cases, they may not want to confront. But these are the areas the Holy Spirit knows they need healing in and wants them to be free so they may continue their spiritual walk with the Lord and not be hindered.

We need God's help in overcoming these areas in our life. He is willing to help us, if we are willing to commit them to the Lord and receive His help. God loves us very much and wants us to overcome all the hindrances that are keeping us from being free so we can accomplish what He has chosen for us to do in our lifetime. Some of these problems may start as far back in our life as conception, and some are passed down from our past generations, either from our parents or grandparents up to the third and fourth generations (Exodus 20: 5).

Rejection

We have found that a great number of Christians have received the spirit of **rejection**, and a lot of it started at their conception due to the fact they were not planned, nor were they really wanted at that time in their parents' lives. Rejection is a spirit and should be cast out of you. Also, sometimes a situation happens making us feel rejected, but it's not a real "spirit of rejection" (even though in our mind we feel like it is). We call this *"self-rejection"* which is a deceiving spirit that deceives us by giving us this false feeling of rejection.

For example, if you were walking down a sidewalk and you pass by some of your friends talking together as you walk past them and they don't acknowledge you or speak to you, this causes you to feel rejected. The truth of the matter is they didn't even see you — but you thought they did. The bottom line is that as you walked by them you didn't speak to them either, even though you saw them. We call this *self-rejection*. This is a deception, but the fact is you rejected them by not speaking to them.

Another area of deception: Satan deceives us, causing us to feel responsible for something that, in reality, we are not responsible for at all. There are many areas of deception but say, for example, that God has given you a ministry to preach or pray for others, and as you continue to do this you start feeling responsible for those you preach to or pray for, especially if you don't see them growing spiritually. You are *only* responsible to accept and function in the ministries and spiritual gifts the Holy Spirit gives to you and that God directs you to do — if you are obedient to His direction, the outcome is God's responsibility. When God's Word goes out, it will accomplish what He sent it out to do.

As we continue on and start looking at some of these things in our lives, remember that not necessarily all the following problems may be hindering you. Everyone is different. We all come from different walks of life and have problems that differ from one another. As you read through the following problems, pray and listen to God's Holy Spirit and He will show you what you should be concerned with. Those are the only one's you should pray about and be concerned with. As we continue on I will cover some of the more prevalent areas where Satan attacks us and hinders our Christian walk.

Please realize that all of our troubles are not necessarily caused by Satan; some of our problems are caused by our own wills and fleshly desires, although Satan's evil spirits cause most of them. He would like for you to believe it's just your character, but in most cases it's one of his evil spirits attacking you trying to deceive and overcome you.

Rebellion

As we continue on and start covering some of the more prevalent spirits that bother us, one of his major spirits is the spirit of "rebellion." This started with Satan when he rebelled against God and when he deceived Adam and Eve. This caused the spirit of rebellion to be passed down to us. We rebel against God by not being obedient to His Word and the direction in which He wants to lead us. The truth of the matter is that most of us just want to do our own thing the way *we* want to do it — this is rebellion.

God created us and put us here on the earth at His appointed time to accomplish His chosen "will" for each of us, and gives us the ability to accomplish it. God gives us special talents and abilities, along with His spiritual gifts and authority to finish the tasks He has chosen for us to do. Although each of us has been given different gifts and talents, they all work together to accomplish God's "will." Sometimes, however, there may be something we don't want to do, so we rebel and procrastinate and don't do it. This is one of the areas that some of us have trouble with which hinders us from going on and accomplishing what God has chosen for us to do.

(1 Samuel 15: 23) — Rebellion is as the sin of witchcraft. When we know God's "will" for us and we refuse to do it, we are in rebellion against God by refusing to be obedient. We are in control of our lives and make our own decision whether or not to be obedient. This is witchcraft control because we are in control of our life rather than allowing God to be in control.

A good example of rebellion is that in my early Christian walk I would tell people that if they could see my past walk with the Lord, they could see two heel prints dug into the ground where God had dragged me along by my collar to get me where He wanted me. This showed me that I was in rebellion, so I cast it out of myself and became more obedient.

Another area that may hinder us is *"inner witchcraft control,"* which is a problem that controls our minds. I will cover this later as we get more into the effects of witchcraft spirits. We as Spirit-filled Christians can expel these spirits by using our *God-given Authority* (Luke 10:19) to cast out evil spirits in ourselves … and in others … if God directs us to do so.

- Confess and repent of the sin of "rebellion" and ask God to forgive you and help you overcome it.
- Speak the following out loud, "Satan, I take authority over your spirit of rebellion, and I tell you to leave me *now*, in the Name of

Jesus Christ!" As you speak this out loud, the spirit of rebellion will have to leave.

Remember, you must always use the Name of "Jesus Christ" when casting out evil spirits, because Jesus defeated Satan and gave us His authority over him. The spirit *has to leave*, but sometimes it helps us to feel better inside if we *continue* to take this authority until we feel relief inside. The spirit has to leave when we command it to leave us, in the Name of Jesus Christ.

Note: When you cast out evil spirits, you may have some kind of a manifestation, but remember Satan doesn't want you to do this. He will try to stop it from happening by using physical manifestations to scare you — hopefully getting you to stop. You may find yourself feeling like crying, coughing, screaming, or sighing ... or you may just feel a relief inside, but don't be afraid. Satan was defeated by Jesus, and we have authority over him. When we use the Name of Jesus Christ, his spirits have to leave.

Through many years of experience we have learned that when you use your God-given authority over Satan, he is like a little puppy dog with a big bark, but no bite. He will do anything he can to keep you from using your authority, so remember, *"He that is in you,* (Jesus) *is greater that he that is in the "world"* (Satan).

Most of the problems we have run into through prayer counseling with others are things that we ourselves have gone through. God uses experiences that we have gone through ourselves to help others.

We have found that if you have gone through experiences yourself and, with God's help, have overcome the problems in your life, you can minister life to people much better than if you were using information or experiences of another person. After you have read this book, have overcome the hindrances in your life and have no further need of it, God may direct you to give it to another person. This book may help others overcome similar problems in their lives that you yourself have gone through and have overcome. If you are willing, God will use all of your experiences and the ways He has helped you to overcome them to help other members in the Body of Christ.

Relationships

There are many problems in our relationships that may be hindering our Christian walk. There are also other areas that won't be covered in this book because people come from so many different lifestyles and God deals with us differently and individually. However, I will cover some of the main problem areas that my wife and I have found in our thirty-four years of ministering to others.

Unforgiveness – Jesus tells us in Luke 11:4 that we need to forgive others so we may receive forgiveness of our sins. Forgiveness is another area where Satan deceives Christians by causing them to think that if they don't forgive the person who has done them wrong, this unforgiveness will have an effect on that person. This is a deception because they are the only ones who will be hurt — not the other person. Sometimes he makes people feel that the sin against them is so bad and hurts them so much, that they can't forgive the person…and they really don't want to! Should you harbor unforgiveness for a long period of time, it may also turn into resentment which may cause you to have physical sickness such as heart problems, arthritis and other problems. Forgiveness is very important to all of us so that we may receive our own forgiveness. It says in the "Lords Prayer" we must forgive others, or God won't forgive our sins.

A few years ago, I was attending a men's prayer meeting where one of the men was recovering from a past heart attack, and was in bad physical shape. He couldn't do much of anything physically, and had to take nitroglycerin to help him function during the day. He requested prayer for healing of his heart, and as we started to pray for him, God showed me that he had resentment against his son, who had caused him and his wife a tremendous amount of trouble in the past. His son had been in all kinds of trouble! The last thing he had done was to steal the family car and gone to South America. I told him that he needed to forgive his son, but he said that he just couldn't because of all the suffering caused by the terrible things his son had done. God led me to ask him if he could pray to the Lord, say that he forgave his son, and ask God to make it real in his heart. After a few minutes of thinking about it and waiting on the Lord, he agreed, and prayed the prayer. We didn't see any thing happen with him that evening, so we adjourned the meeting until the following week. When we came together the next week, we could see a great change in his countenance, and he was full of joy. He shared what had happened to him — that God had healed his heart. He could now mow his yard and do things that he hadn't been able to do since his heart attack, and he didn't need to take any nitroglycerin to do so. He shared that he had forgiven his son and that he was free of the unforgiveness. We all praised the Lord and gave God the glory for his healing. As we walk with the Lord, it is necessary that we keep short accounts, forgiving others for their wrongdoings so we may be forgiven for ours. Unforgiveness opens spiritual doors for other evil spirits such as "anger," "hate," "resentment" and sometimes "murder" to enter in; so, for our own protection, we must keep short accounts and forgive others. Remember that *forgiving* someone is a **decision** that each of us has to make. It doesn't have anything to do with the way we feel towards the other person. We decide to forgive the person and speak the words, "I forgive the person for whatever." Then God changes our hearts and makes it real to us.

The Bible says that we should love and pray for our enemies, even though we don't like the sin in which they are involved. Sometimes it helps if, in our mind, we are able to separate the sin the person is involved in from the person that Jesus loved and died for. If we can do that, we can also love the person.

Our bodies are called *temples of God's Holy Spirit*, and if our bodies are temples, they can hold things inside just like physical temples or churches do. If our temples should hold any evil thing or evil spirits, we must get rid of them so our walk with the Lord won't be hindered. Jesus did this when He came back into Jerusalem and ran the "money changers" out of the temple. He cleansed the temple of evil! If our temples have evil things (spirits) in them, we must cast them out so we will be clean and able to hold more of Jesus and God's Holy Spirit. This is called **"deliverance"** because it *cleanses* our temples. So, when we ask to be filled with God's Holy Spirit, we now have more room in our temples to hold more of God's Holy Spirit Who fills us with His power and enables us to overcome the temptation and problems we may face in the future.

Another very important area of our Christian walk is **"forgiveness"** — after we have forgiven other people whom we have had anger or resentment toward, and have repented and asked God to forgive us, we need to forgive ourselves for our sins. We have found that some people don't realize that if we can't forgive ourselves for things we have done, then in actuality we are playing god because God has already forgiven us of our sins — and who are we that we can't forgive ourselves! The fact of the matter is that if we can't forgive ourselves, it is *impossible* to love ourselves, whom Jesus loves and for whom He gave His life.

Sins of the Past Generations – We read in the book of Exodus (20:5) that it is possible that people may suffer from sins and curses that were passed down from our past generations through our blood lines. These are not sins that we have committed but, never-the-less, it's possible that we, and our children, may be having problems because of them. For example, let's look at people where there has been a divorce in their family. If we were to look at their past generations, we would probably see divorce in their past blood lines, as well. Divorce isn't the only thing that could be passed down to us through our past generations; there could also be addictions, sexual sins, occult and many other problems. These sins and curses can be eliminated through effective warfare prayers. We have God's authority to do this, and as you use His authority you will find that the problems associated with these sins will stop. We need to pray using God's Word as a sword and "cut ourselves free" from any sins and curses that have come down from the blood lines of our past generations, up to and including the third and fourth generations on our mother's side and our father's side of our family. When we use the term "cut" it is using it as the "Sword of the Spirit" which is the Word of God.

Remember that we also have a mind of own, and we can choose to enter into these sins ourselves. If this has happened in our past, we need to pray, using the Word of God to "cut our children free" from those sins that we have committed so they won't be affected by our sins being passed down to them.

Prayer Example – Pray, "I take the authority given to me in Luke 10:19 and cut myself free from the sins of my past generations on my father's side of my family up through the fourth generation, and in Jesus' Name, I release myself from all curses and evil spirits that came down to me through these blood lines. I 'bind' these curses and evil spirits and I 'command' them to leave in Jesus' Name." Pray *specific* prayers, and after you have felt the release from them, you should pray and do the same thing over your mother's side of her family up through the fourth generation. Some people really get a huge release from this prayer. Remember, if you have children, you should also pray over them and do the same thing, setting them free, so they won't be hindered in their spiritual walk with the Lord.

Marriage Problems

Inability to communicate with our spouses can cause many other problems, such as anger, resentment and rejection. Lack of communication, in most cases, is not an evil spirit but is of the flesh, and to overcome this you need to ask God's help. You should also ask your spouse for forgiveness and make a commitment to start communicating with each other and with God's help, you will! We have found that an individual who is "self-centered" may have a communication problem; but it's possible that it is caused by something else and with God's help it, too, can be overcome.

God created man and woman differently in many respects and the physical and spiritual needs of the woman are much different from the needs of the man. Women require their husbands to share things with them and express love — not only sexually, but through hugging, kissing, caressing and continually telling her that he loves her. Women also feel things in the Spirit usually before the husband does. It's as though she has her antenna out and she picks up things in the Spirit before her husband does. This is one of the reasons that the husband needs to listen to his wife, so that he may hear God's guidance and direction. As he listens to what his wife says, a husband can discern what is from the Lord and make the right decision.

There are many other ways that God speaks to you, but this is one of the ways husbands miss God's directions at times because he doesn't want to hear what his wife is saying. If your wife says to you, "I think that we should do so and so" or "I feel like we shouldn't do that," don't disregard what she is saying as it may be God's answer or direction for you.

When a couple is married they become as one in the flesh; but God also wants them to become "one in the Spirit," and when they become as "one" they become very powerful in the Lord. It takes both the husband and the wife to be a whole. If this isn't happening in a marriage, the family is missing half of itself and isn't nearly as powerful in the Lord as they could be.

Sex Problems – Some problems in this area may be caused by physical problems, but most of the time they are caused by Satan's evil spirits. It can be a "perverted spirit" that came from our past generations, or it may have come through something that may have happened to us in our past or that we have allowed ourselves to get involved in. The spirits of "lust of the flesh" and "pornography" are two of the most prevalent spirits that Satan uses against us to tempt us to commit sin.

However, the spirit of "lust of power and of things of the world" is very prevalent also. We want new cars, new clothes, new boats and many other things, which are fine — unless they overpower us and we become obsessed with these desires. Material things that we have may be blessings from the Lord, but if we spend too much time thinking about them or playing with them, we may become *obsessed* with them and drawn away from the Lord — possibly drawn into the sin of idolatry. God loves us and wants to bless us mightily and He wants us to be obedient and put Him first in our lives. But we can miss a lot of His blessings if we allow Satan to rob us through our "lack of knowledge" and by not using the authority that God gives us through Jesus Christ to overcome Satan in our lives (Luke 10:19).

The spirit of **"homosexuality"** (either male or female) is also a strong spirit that affects some Christian marriage relationships. Through the "spirit of deception" and lack of knowledge of the scriptures, some people accept practices in their sex life that are against the Word of God. In the Bible, Leviticus18:22 tells us that a man shouldn't lay with another man as a woman. Leviticus 20:13 says that this act is an *abomination* – and the person was put to death! There is a deception of some people with the scripture that says the marriage bed is undefiled, and this is true, if we can also accept the scripture in 1 Thessalonians 4:4 which tells us that we should know how to possess our vessel in sanctification and honor. The scripture in Romans 1: 24-27 cautions us against changing the natural use of our bodies into that which is against nature.

While ministering with people, we were surprised to find that so many of God's Christians were having "oral sex," thinking that it was okay due to the scripture that says that the marriage bed is undefiled. But practically every woman who confessed this as a practice in her marriage was having problems. It was causing them trouble in their sex life, and they didn't like it. It is not the natural way that God created us to have sex, and they were deceived into thinking that it was okay. Homosexuals, both men and women are deceived into thinking that they were born that way and that it is natural for them. This isn't true — it is an evil spirit and they can be set free from it — if they so choose. Oral sex is also a homosexual spirit and it can be cast out if the person wants to be free.

Adultery – This is a sin that Satan uses against Christians to tempt them when they find themselves in the wrong place at the wrong time. If you get involved with someone of the opposite sex, it is your decision to do so, but you can overcome this lustful temptation with the power of God's Holy Spirit. Although the grass may look greener on the other side of the fence, it can lead you to your spiritual death. Genesis 2:24 tells us that when you have sex with someone, you become as "one" and when this happens, it is possible to take on evil spirits that the other person may have. If this has happened in your life, you should confess it to God as sin and ask His forgiveness. Then you should take authority over this spirit of "adultery" and cast it out using the Name of Jesus.

Fornication – This sin of having sex outside of marriage affects a large percentage of our younger generation today. This usually happens when a young person is growing up in their teenage years before marriage, but may also happen to a person who's been divorced. In the world today, "fornication" is very prevalent with a number of young people who are planning to get married later, but who choose to live together first, before marriage. There are a number of Christians who choose this type of lifestyle, who may not know it is a sin, or who may choose to do it anyway. In one way, the results are similar to adultery in the fact that you can pick up evil spirits from the other person which may affect you later in your marriage.

If you have had sex with someone other than the person you marry, it can affect your sexual relationship with your future spouse because as you are having sex with your spouse, you may be fantasizing in your subconscious mind that you are having sex with someone else. It is possible for you to get all kinds of evil and unclean spirits — especially lust, which may cause problems with your marriage. Lust draws you into many other areas, such as pornography, sexual fantasy, masturbation, and other areas. Lust is also a spirit that is never satisfied and continually tries to take you further into the sin in which you are involved. To rid yourself of these spirits, you should r*epent* … *confess* each act as sin … then *ask* for God's forgiveness and He will forgive you.

In 1 Corinthians 6: 9, the Bible tells us that if we are involved in any of these sins, we shall not inherit the Kingdom of God. After repenting, you should take your authority by using the Word of God as a sword, and cut yourself free from that person or persons with whom you have been involved in your past. Take the authority given to you by Jesus and cast these spirits of "fornication, lust, and all other unclean spirits" out of yourself. Remember, *He that is within you is greater than he that is in the world.*

Incest – The sin of having sex with someone in your family, such as your brother, sister or one of your parents. This generally takes place with younger children as they are growing up and wanting to experiment with each other. In rare cases it happens with one of the parents, but usually it is with a brother or a sister. If this has happened to you, you should treat it like any other sexual sin. Confess it as sin, repent and cast the spirit of "incest" out of yourself.

Sodomy – The act of having un-natural sexual intercourse with persons of the same sex, especially males, or with an animal. When this happened in the Old Testament (Exodus 22: 19), the people were put to death; but with Jesus, we can be forgiven for this sin. If you have committed this sin, you should repent and ask God to forgive you and cast the spirit of sodomy out of yourself.

Perversion – Any sexual act that doesn't conform to the way God created us to have sexual intercourse. This covers a multitude of things that Satan uses to tempt Christians to get involved in — especially if they have a spirit of "lust." He uses a multitude of things to do this, such as X and R-rated movies, internet, e-mails, VHS and DVD movies, TV shows, magazines, and other types of pornography to draw people into perverted sexual activity. It is especially hard for our young people today to overcome all the temptations Satan uses to tempt them to get them involved in acts of perversion and other sexual sins; but with the power of God's Holy Spirit, your authority and praying in "Jesus' Name," *you can overcome them.* You have to rebuke the spirit of "perversion," cast it out of yourself and ask God to give you help to overcome future temptations.

Rape – Rape is not the sin of the person, but of the attacker. This doesn't require God to forgive you; however, as hard as it may be, you need to forgive the person who raped you. Remember, you don't have to *feel like* forgiving the person because forgiveness is a *decision.* When you decide to forgive the person, God will make it real in your heart. Remember, we have to forgive so we can receive God's forgiveness. It is a terrible thing when a person or child has been raped or molested by someone; however, the victim can be healed through prayers. *Nothing is impossible with our loving God.*

If you have been a victim of rape, you need to pray and ask God to remove any germs that you may have encountered, and to heal your body and mind of the physical trauma that you received through the terrible incident. You also need to cast out all the unclean spirits that may have entered into you from the person, including the spirit of "lust." It may take a little time for you to recover from the thoughts and fear that you encountered, but you can pray the scripture in 2 Corinthians 10:5, *bringing your thoughts under the obedience of Christ Jesus,* and this will help.

Masturbation – The act of masturbation will open the door for the spirits of fantasy, pornography and lust to enter into you. This isn't the natural way God created us to have sex. It's a form of "self-gratification" and also becomes very addictive and should not be practiced. If you have been involved in this, you should repent; ask God's forgiveness, cast out the spirit of masturbation and other spirits that go along with it. When it has gone, you should pray and ask God to help you to overcome this act should the temptation come back and, if it does, you will have a split second to decide which way you will go. Commit it to the Lord, ask God for strength to overcome the temptation, and He will help you to overcome. If you should find that you have slipped and masturbated again, *repent again!* Ask God to forgive you and to give you more strength to overcome the temptation in the future. Don't listen to Satan who may be telling you that your deliverance didn't work, that you might as well forget it and to continue doing your thing. He will try to rob you if he can get you to believe that.

Unholy Dreams – Your mind is the battlefield and sometimes Satan can cause you to have weird dreams, especially when you forget to pray and commit yourself to the Lord before you go to sleep. I have found that in your prayer time before going to sleep, if you will commit your "body, mind, and spirit" into the Lord's hands and ask for His protection while you sleep, these dreams will usually stop. When you are asleep your body sleeps, but your spirit doesn't. This is the time that Satan's people may be praying curses on us. You may even wake up and be afraid to open your eyes because you feel, in your spirit, that something is standing next to your bed. In most cases, if you commit your body, soul and spirit into the Lord's hands before you go to sleep, these thoughts will stop and you will sleep much better.

When you are baptized with the Holy Spirit, you become more susceptible to the spirit world, and Satan will try to scare you with these things. But you shouldn't be afraid of him because you have the authority of God in you and you can tell him to leave you alone…"In Jesus Name."

Other Hindrances of Evil Spirits

Usually in Groups
- Hate, Anger, Murder and Self Destruction
- Lust, Pornography, Fantasies, Masturbation, and Perversion
- Addictions (Many Types)
- Witchcraft and Rebellion

Emotional Problems
- Rejection
- Self Pity (Wounded Spirit)
- Depression / Despair
- Anxiety / Stress
- Jealousy

Mental Problems
- Confusion
- Doubt
- Double Minded
- Schizophrenia and Mental Torment
- Witchcraft / Rebellion

- Occult Involvement
- Generational Sins
- Chemical

Speech Problems
- Lies
- Blasphemy
- Judgment / Criticism / Gossip
- Cursing and Profanity

Religious Errors
- False Religions / Cults / Unbelief
- Religious Traditions of Man / Deception
- Eastern Religions, Mormonism, Christian Science, Jehovah Witness, Humanism, and Islam: All are religions that do not believe that Jesus Christ is the Son of God and the only way to the Father God, and that we receive salvation by accepting Jesus Christ as our Savior.

Occult Areas

Deuteronomy 18:10–12,
1 Samuel 15:23,
Exodus: 4–5

Most people, whether serious or not, have at some time in their past lifestyle been involved in some area of the occult. People, through their curiosity and lack of knowledge, get involved in these areas not knowing the seriousness of the consequences and the effects they may have on them later in life.

(Hosea 4: 6) My people perish for lack of knowledge. Satan is a legalist and when you get involved in the occult, he has a legal claim on you. For example, a large percentage of Christians have at sometime in their lives read their horoscope, and when asked why, most people will say, "Well I just wanted to see how close it would come to reality in my life." These readings are projected into your sub-conscious mind

and you program your life to happen according to what they say — either good or bad. If it says that you are going to have a good day ... or a bad day, you unconsciously program yourself to have that kind of day.

(Revelation 12:10) *Satan is the destroyer and the accuser of the brethren.* Some other areas of the occult that trouble a number of Christians are "palm reading," "fortune telling," "ouija boards," "astrology," and "eastern religions." If you have been involved in any of these occult areas, you need to renounce them —and all the information that you received through these practices—by speaking out loud to Satan renouncing each of the individual areas that you have been involved in. Then pray to God confessing them as sin and ask God to forgive you for each area of involvement. You see, there are two "powers" that you can get information from: Satan or God. So, if you are trying to get information from any way other than God, you are trying to get it through Satan or his evil spirits. There are many other areas in the occult, but I only covered some of the more prevalent areas that seem to hinder people in their Christian walk.

Witchcraft – This is one of the more prevalent and active controlling spirits Satan uses against Christians today, and is used in many areas of our churches, families, relationships, and businesses. Many families are affected by this controlling witchcraft spirit, which has destroyed many marriage relationships by operating through either the husband or wife. Children often have a controlling spirit which robs and controls a lot of family functions.

(1 Sam.15:23) Witchcraft is as this sin of rebellion, and we are born with the sin of rebellion, which was the original sin that started with Adam and Eve in the Garden of Eden. They rebelled against God and ate the fruit after God had told them not to eat of the fruit of the "Tree of Good and Evil." In Genesis 3:6, Eve ate the fruit first, and then gave some to Adam and he ate, also. Witchcraft causes people to want to be in control of things and other people, usually because of "lust for power" — or else they just want to be in charge of *everything*.

Witchcraft in the Church – I believe that Satan uses this to cause more trouble in our churches than any other evil spirit, with the exception of gossip and back-biting, which has caused splits in many churches.

This spirit of **witchcraft** is also known as a *controlling spirit* while some may call it a *"Jezebel"* spirit, but it's the spirit of witchcraft. In the church, it's usually a person or persons working together, having a spirit of "lust for power" and wanting to be in control of the functions in the church. It can be male or female, but it wants to be in control of everything. This spirit that tries to control the minister in what he/she does and how he/she preaches, is very critical, and finds fault with the way things are done by the preacher and is very deceptive in many ways in order to get its own way. It may either be a person with large financial gifts who supports the church, or a very domineering person who wants to be on all the different boards that control the church.

In some cases it is the pastor or his wife who is supposed to be in control of the church, but who is not open to hear God's direction – neither from the Holy Spirit nor through other mature Christians in their Body of Christ who are Spirit-filled and who have God's wisdom.

This is a very alluring and deceiving spirit. People who have it are usually unaware that they have it, and think they are helping in their areas of involvement. In most cases, people won't recognize that they are operating without God's gift of "Discerning of Spirits." Most all churches either have, or have had, problems with this spirit of control. In some cases, it has stifled the Holy Spirit from working; in other cases, it has caused a split in their church.

Witchcraft in the Family — It is a very prevailing spirit that Satan uses to create problems in our family relations. It could be the wife, husband or a child, who is very knowledgeable in controlling circum-stances to get his/her way by crying, pouting, yelling, lying, or by many other ways which include manip-ulation, money and gifts, to achieve control. They learn very fast what to do and how to do it!. Many families have been divorced because of this control-ling spirit! In some cases, it has prevented them from accomplishing "God's will" in their lives and keeps their family from being in God's "spiritual order." This witchcraft spirit may also prevent them from receiving God's blessings, and will certainly prevent them from being "strong in the Spirit" because they are not in one accord when they pray together.

Witchcraft in Yourself — Through experience, we have learned that we are sometimes hindered from accomplishing "God's will" in our own lives because of images we have created in our sub-conscious minds as to how we should act, and what we should do when we are in certain situations. In explaining this, it is like a little form, or image of ourselves in our sub-conscious mind that may appear to have been cut out with a little cookie cutter of a gingerbread man. This image is formed in our sub-conscious mind by things that have taken place in the past in our lives. In most cases, it may come from things we have been taught by school teachers, from religious teachings or traditions of man, and peer pressures from our friends. It makes us try to fit ourselves into this image of ourselves, which is reflected in the way we act when we go to church, or when we are around other people. Some may call this "putting up a front," but in reality it is "inner witchcraft control" as we try to make ourselves fit into this image, or by the way we act in certain situations in our lives.

This spirit prevents you from being "free" to do what God wants you to do, and causes you to get frustrated when you don't fit into this sub-conscious image which you think, according to your intellect, is perfect. So, if you think any of these areas of witchcraft are in your life and hindering your walk with the Lord, repent and ask God to forgive you. Commit this area of your mind to the Lord, and cast this inner witchcraft control out of yourself. Then ask God to show you this spirit if it tries to return in the future, so that you may rebuke it and keep it away from you.

Projections/Fiery Darts — Controlling thought projections are used in many ways to control others in order to gain something — either in business or to attain favors from someone. It is a very powerful spirit and if you are under this control, you may not know it until the person(s) with this spirit have attained their way. Although, if *you* have the spiritual gift of God's discernment, you may feel in your spirit that something is wrong. Sometimes, it might make you feel that your "mind" has stopped working and you can't think clearly. If this should happen to you, pray and commit yourself to the Lord immediately and bring your mind under the obedience of Christ Jesus according to the scripture in 2 Corinthians 10:5. Take authority over all projections that are coming against you; tell them to "stop (!) ...in the Name of Jesus" and they will stop. It helps if you are dressed in God's full armor in accordance with Ephesians 6:12.

Some people who are in Satan worship have the ability to project a spirit of control toward other people in order to get their way and desires. Also, there are many Christians who pray wrongful prayers for others that become projections toward that person. They may mean well, but pray their own will and not according to the Word of God. I consider all of these types of projections to be "fiery darts" that are mentioned in Ephesians 6:13, which tells us we should dress ourselves in the "full armor of God." Being obedient to do this will help protect us against projections coming at us through this spirit. Remember, *we fight not against flesh and blood, but against spiritual wickedness in high places.*

Repentance and Deliverance

If you should find that you have been involved in any areas of sin, and you want to overcome them in your life, you need to repent of them to God, confess them as sin and ask God's forgiveness. **Repentance** is being *sorry* for the sins we have committed in our past, or that we are presently involved in, knowing they are against God's Word, and believing that with God's help we will overcome them. When we confess our sins to God and repent of them, they are covered with the Blood of Jesus — God doesn't see them anymore.

Deliverance – Deliverance is something that Satan doesn't want us Christians to know about, or to do, because it destroys the work he has done to defeat us and to kill us spiritually if he can. Deliverance is a battle in the Spirit where we are fighting against evil spirits that we can't physically see with our eyes. But we must remember that God is also Spirit and we can't see Him either. Never-the-less, they are both real!

The spirit world is more real than the physical world that we live in; even though we can't see it, it can control us spiritually. When we pray or take authority over Satan and his evil spirits, we are fighting in the spirit, doing **spiritual warfare**.

(Ephesians 6:12) *We do not war against flesh and blood, but against "powers and principalities, and rulers of darkness"* which are evil spirits that Satan uses to defeat us. He uses "fear" and "lack of knowledge" trying to prevent us from using **Spiritual Warfare** against him.

(Mark 16:17-18) Tells us that as believers, we should all be *"casting out evil spirits, speaking with new tongues and healing the sick,"* but most Christians are not doing this due to "lack of knowledge," "fear," or "unbelief." Christians, in a lot of cases, are not using their *spiritual authority* that Jesus gave them to overcome Satan in their lives and in their families; therefore, he is having a hay-day attacking them in many ways. (Luke 10-19) *Jesus gave us the authority over all the power of the enemy,* but sometimes we fail to use it.

Jesus is our example of how we, as Christians, should be. He cast out evil spirits many times, and He wants us to do the same so that we may live a good life overcoming things that hinder us. When you pray deliverance over yourself, you have to pray using the name of "Jesus" or it will be ineffective and the spirits won't leave. You see, we don't have the power ourselves, but when we use the Name of "Jesus," our words are powerful because Jesus gave us His authority. Satan was defeated when Jesus went to the "cross" and when He arose three days later.

Also, when these spirits are in the process of being "cast out," Satan may cause things to happen to scare you and, hopefully, to get you to stop because they don't want to leave. Before you start casting them out, you should speak out loud and *"bind them in the Name of Jesus,"* which in most cases will stop the manifestations as they are expelled. An example of this is would be to say, "I bind the spirit of __ (?)__ in me and I command you to come out quietly in Jesus' Name." You don't have to be afraid of these manifestations because they won't hurt you, but they do want you to stop.

When an evil spirit is being cast out, you may hear it say things back to you such as, "I am not coming out, this is my home" or "if you don't stop, I am going to kill you!" Or you may hear "screaming" or "coughing" — but don't believe what they say. You shouldn't carry on a conversation with them, but you should continue to tell them to leave in "Jesus' Name" until you feel some relief inside. Do not give up because they have got to leave when you use the name of "Jesus" Who defeated Satan, Who loved us enough to sacrifice His life for us, Who died on the Cross and arose three days later, ascending into Heaven.

In most cases you will feel some relief after the "casting out" is complete, but you may feel weak and have little energy left. This is a normal feeling because you have just gone through spiritual surgery. At this time, you need to pray for the Holy Spirit to fill you and give you God's peace and joy.

Remember when Jesus ran the money changers out of the temple, He delivered the temple of the evil that had taken up abode there. This is the same as our temples being delivered when we cast the evil spirits out of ourselves in Jesus' Name. Our temples are also being cleansed of the evil. After our deliverance, we should always pray for an in-filling of God's Holy Spirit to prevent these evil spirits from being able to return, bringing others with them and causing us to be worse than we were in the beginning. If we are full of God's Holy Spirit, there isn't room in our temples for them to come back.

Cleansing of our Homes and Other Buildings — Sometimes you may need to go through your home or office and cleanse the evil spirits out of them. When you enter your home or certain rooms in your home or office, you may feel some evil presence lingering there. This is sometimes prevalent with the "mischievous" spirits that may cause things to move or fall off the wall, or that cause noises in the house. The Germans call them Poltergeist, and Satan uses them to frighten us. They may live in buildings due to the curses that were put on them during their construction. There are several examples of how this may happen.

There was a curse put on the ground in the book of Genesis — everything that we use in construction comes from the ground. Also during construction, men who are in the process of building structures sometimes curse the materials they are using to build with, and this is one of the ways that doors open for Satan's spirits to come in and abide there. We sometimes bring items into our home that may have curses on them from someone. Also, astrology items and things used in occult practices should be removed from your home because these are ways that doors open for Satan to come into your homes and offices.

If you should notice things of this nature happening in your home or office, you should commit your home or office and everything in them, to God. Ask Him to show you, as you walk through each room, if there are any items that are not right and which you should remove.

After removing these items, go through each room and take authority over all evil spirits and curses that may have been put on the furniture and other items during construction or manufacturing. Tell the evil spirits to leave "in the Name of Jesus," and they will leave.

You should also take authority and tell the spirits in all the utility systems to leave, because sometimes the spirits may cause these systems to break or stop working. Additionally, if there has been a death in the home, you should cast out the spirit of "death," and "infirmity." After the cleansing is complete, you should ask God to fill your home or office with his Holy Spirit, His presence, His peace and Joy.

Infilling of God's Holy Spirit

In the world today, it's especially necessary for us to have the power of God's Holy Spirit in us so we can overcome the worldly pressures and temptations that we are confronted with each day. It says in John 14:17 that it was necessary for Jesus to go to the Father so that He could send the Holy Spirit to us, and He shall be **with** us and He shall be **in** us. When we accept our salvation, it is because God's Holy Spirit is with us, drawing us to the Lord and convicting us, so that we will accept Jesus as our Savior. When we are baptized with God's Holy Spirit, not only is God's Holy Spirit with us, but He enters into us and lives in us.

When we pray and ask the Father to baptize us with his Holy Spirit according to the scripture in Luke 11:11, God's Holy Spirit comes in and dwells in us. When this happens, God's Holy Spirit gives us spiritual gifts according to 1 Corinthians 12. These gifts are *God's power gifts* for us to use in ministering to others. One of the spiritual gifts that everyone needs, along with the baptism of the Holy Spirit, is the *manifestation of the Holy Spirit,* which is the *spiritual language* that God gives us. Most people call this gift "Speaking in Tongues" which God gives each of us personally.

In the past, this gift has caused trouble in the Body of Christ because some people, even though they have prayed to be filled with God's Holy Spirit, have not been able to receive the manifestation. This could be due to several things.

It seems to be more difficult for persons blessed with highly intellectual minds because they have a need to understand the spiritual gift; but it is impossible for us to understand a lot of things of the spirit with our intellects. We have to accept some of the spiritual things *with faith* and not with our intellects. For us to speak in this God-given language, we have to bypass our thoughts in our mind, and let the sounds come out of our mouth. God showed me that it is like a baby trying to learn to walk. It's hard for a baby to take the first step, because it doesn't know how. We don't know how to speak in this language either because we don't understand it with our minds; and with some highly intellectual people, it is even more difficult. When we pray and ask God to baptize us with His Holy Spirit, He does in accordance with the scripture in Luke 11:11, and we receive the Holy Spirit along with the gift of tongues at the same time. You just have to start speaking it, which is very humbling—speaking things that, in your mind, you don't understand. But keep trying until you can speak it out.

This is a personal gift from God to us and we need this for our own spiritual strength and welfare. The Bible tells us (John 14:16-17) that God's Holy Spirit is our Comforter and a Spirit of Truth. When we pray in this language, we are blessed inside, and it makes us feel good spiritually. Also in Romans 8:26, the Bible tells us that when we pray in the Spirit, the Holy Spirit intercedes for us and prays the *perfect prayer* for whatever the need may be. Sometimes, we know of a prayer need, but we don't know what the problem is or how to pray. If we pray in our prayer language, *it will be the perfect prayer* for that problem because the Holy Spirit will be praying through us.

When we receive God's Holy Spirit, our spiritual understanding is opened and we begin to understand more of the scriptures and their spiritual meaning better than we did before. The Bible tells us that we, as Spirit-filled Christians can discern the things of the world, but the people of the world cannot discern the Spiritual things. The Bible tells us that we should worship God in "Spirit and in Truth," and we accomplish this by *praying in the Spirit* and *singing in the Spirit.*

Healing of our Spirit, Soul and Body

As we read these Bible scriptures, (Isaiah 53:4-6, 1 Pet.2:24, James 5:16, 3 John 1:2). we learn that it's God's will that we be healed in our bodies and minds. We do not understand why sometimes when we pray for people they are healed, and other times they don't receive their healing; but I believe that, in some cases, there are certain hindrances that prevent us from receiving God's healing. We continue to ask Jesus to do something that He has already done. The scripture says that we are healed through the stripes that Jesus took before going to the Cross. That says to me that we are healed in the spirit, but we have to receive it physically. The provisions for our healing have been taken care of by the stripes that Jesus took. When He said *"It is finished,"* everything that we needed to receive by His healing in our bodies and spirits was completed. I also believe our healing can be blocked by "doubt and unbelief." Sometimes, for some reason, a person doesn't want to be healed. Remember when Jesus asked the man if he wanted to be healed at the pool of Bethesda before He healed him? Sometimes we pray, asking God to heal a person in the way we perceive to be right for that person; but in reality we are putting God in a box by asking Him to do it our way, which is praying amiss. When the person receives healing, it may be in a completely different way than the way we thought or hoped it would be done. We always want instant healings, but sometimes God wants to heal a person through doctors or through medication.

We know God loves us and wants us to be in good health, but I believe that a more perfect way would be to pray that the person could receive the healing that Jesus took the stripes for, and that God's highest will would be accomplished in the person's body. We should also speak to the person's body (temple) and tell it to **receive** God's healing according to the scripture which says *we are healed by the stripes of Jesus*. Our words are powerful and creative when we use the scripture — Jesus is the Word, and when we speak the Word, it is powerful and creative! Remember God spoke the Word and created the world and all that is within it. Our word is also creative when we speak negative things so, as Christians, we *must* watch what we say.

Full Armor of God

The Bible says in Ephesians 6:13-18 *to take up the Whole Armor of God, that you may be able to withstand in the evil day, and having done all to stand.*

Although we are protected through Jesus, we have learned that it helps to do this every day before we get started for the day.

- Breastplate of Righteousness
- Shod your feet with the preparation of the Gospel of Peace
- Shield of Faith to quench all the fiery darts of the wicked one
- Helmet of Salvation
- Sword of the Spirit, which is the Word of God

Pray always with all prayer and supplication in the Spirit, being watchful to this end with all perseverance and supplication for the Saints.

New Commitments

This is the time for making new commitments. God wants us to commit every part of our lives to Him so He can be in charge of them. When we receive Christ in our lives and ask Him to forgive us for all of our sins, He forgives us; but He is not the Lord of many areas of our lives until we commit them to Him and ask Him to be the Lord of each area. When we do this, He begins to work in these areas to help us overcome certain things that we are doing wrong as Christians. This is the way we grow spiritually closer to the Lord and "die to ourselves," making Him Lord over each of these areas. Dying to self daily is a continual process in our life if we desire to grow closer to the Lord.

Walking out
Deliverance

After we receive our deliverance, we need to realize that we also have a part to play in order to keep it. We certainly want to keep our deliverance and not allow the spirits to return! If this were to happen, we would be worse off now than we were in the beginning (Matt.12:35). The difference after we are delivered, and if the temptation comes back, is that the Holy Spirit gives us a split second to decide what to do – whether to yield to the temptation or not to yield. The Holy Spirit gives us power to overcome our temptations, but we have *to want* to overcome them.

Sometimes it may take awhile to completely overcome the problem because along with it, we may also have to overcome a physical habit. For example, if our problem is smoking and we have already cast out the spirit of "addiction to nicotine," we may still have to overcome *the habit* of reaching for a cigarette without thinking what we are doing. As we continue to pray and seek God's help to overcome this habit, we know that He *will* help us. However, if we should find ourselves back doing the same thing from which we were delivered, it doesn't necessarily mean the spirit has come back again. But if we *willfully continue* in the problem, it *will* come back. After we have been set free, we must *resist the devil and he will flee*.

God loves us so much that He sent his Son Jesus into the world, not only for our salvation, but to set us free from all the oppression that Satan has afflicted us with. Not only does God want to bless us more than we could ever imagine or comprehend, but also for us Christians to commit all areas of our lives to Him so we can grow closer to Him.